FaithBuilders #7—
Straight as a String

FaithBuilders #7—
Straight as a String

. . . and Other Bible Lessons for Kids

C. W. Bess

Baker Books

A Division of Baker Book House Co
Grand Rapids, Michigan 49516

Published by Baker Books
a division of Baker Book House Company
P.O. Box 6287, Grand Rapids, MI 49516-6287

New paperback edition published 2001

Previously published as *Sparkling Object Sermons for Children*

Printed in the United States of America

ISBN 0-8010-6371-X

Scripture quotations are from the Revised Standard Version of the Bible, copyright 1946, 1952, 1971 by the Division of Christian Education of the National Council of the Churches of Christ in the USA. Used by permission.

For current information about all releases from Baker Book House, visit our web site:

http://www.bakerbooks.com

Contents

1 Rebellion and Redemption   7
2 Who Does God Love Most?   10
3 Straight as a String   12
4 Sealed by the Holy Spirit   14
5 The Unopened Letter   16
6 Sin and Scars   18
7 The Best Training of All   20
8 Look Inside   22
9 How to Handle the Truth   24
10 Tongues and Toothpaste   26
11 Push—Not Pull   28
12 Good Punishment   30
13 On the Level with God   32
14 Magic Beans?   34
15 Self-control   36
16 Power   38
17 Something Is Missing   40
18 Judgment Day Coming   42
19 What Color Is the Rainbow?   44
20 Life the Second Time   46
21 The Perfect Tool   48
22 Do as I Say?   50
23 A Time for Every Purpose   52
24 How to Wake Up   54
25 Turtles and Tents   56
26 God Sees All   58
27 Trust in the Lord   60
28 All Treasure and No Trash   62
29 Strangers to the Spirit   64

30 Give Up?   66

31 Giving Back to God   68

32 You Can't Hide from God   70

33 What's Inside?   72

34 Beautiful Feet   74

35 How to See Yourself?   76

36 First Fruits or Last Crumbs?   78

37 Time for Beauty   80

38 Trained by Patience   82

39 Trees for Toothpicks and Telephone Poles   84

40 The Whole Armor of God   86

41 Brave as a Lion   88

42 The One-eyed Monster   90

43 The Magic Glasses   92

44 Tell the Whole World   94

1 Rebellion and Redemption

Interest Object: The name Itisi printed on one side of a piece of cardboard or poster board and "It is I" on the other

Main Truth: Jesus paid for our sins to buy us back.

Scripture Text: "But God shows his love for us in that while we were yet sinners Christ died for us" (Rom. 5:8).

"A man owned a dog named Itisi (pronounced I-tis-e) which he loved very much. [Show sign with correct spelling.] He fed Itisi well and trained him to be obedient. However, Itisi became restless and longed for total freedom instead of obedience. He didn't want anyone to tell him what to do.

"The master recognized that temptation and could have tied his dog to a tree, but who wants a dog chained like a criminal? That's no fun for the dog. Neither is it a joy for the owner if he can't trust his own dog. Therefore, he decided to let Itisi make the choice. The dog was not locked up but was given freedom in the back yard. Only when they walked in the neighborhood was the leash used.

"Sure enough. One day Itisi decided to escape by jumping over the fence. He never noticed that his collar caught on the fence and tore off. His master's name was no longer on his neck.

"Itisi roamed the alleys and the streets confident that his new life was better than his past. He didn't worry about the damage he caused in Mrs. Smith's garden. So what if he tore open bags of garbage? Who cared if he scattered trash while seeking food from Mr. Jones' garbage cans?

"Itisi thought it funny how angry the neighborhood mothers became when he pulled their laundry from clotheslines. He enjoyed his freedom and learned bad things from new friends in his dog pack. Now he didn't have to obey anyone! He could do anything he wanted.

"In those days Itisi did not realize that his once sleek fur was becoming shabby. No longer was he the clean and healthy dog of his past. He had changed! With no owner to discipline him or love him, Itisi was a different dog.

"One day Itisi needed the leash that wasn't there anymore. He had played too rough with some mean children, and before he knew what happened he bit a boy. Angry neighbors cornered him and soon the dogcatcher carried him to the pound where he awaited death.

"Itisi had broken all the rules. Now he had to pay for his sins. His only hope was the master he had fled. But he couldn't escape to run home and plead for help. Itisi couldn't even tell the dogcatcher his master's name. If only he still had his collar on which was written his master's name. How proud he would be to wear it again.

"Now it seemed too late. Tomorrow he must die! If only his master could find and rescue him. The end was near.

"Then he heard the wonderful sound of familiar footsteps. It was indeed his master! The man was very sad as he looked down on his beloved dog. He hardly recognized this thin, dirty dog. Would he be willing to pay a big price to redeem Itisi? He was!

"Now it was Itisi's turn to decide. The dogcatcher explained the plan. Itisi must accept the leash and obey his master. If not, he must die. And of course, Itisi decided to accept the pardon on those terms.

"In the story whom does the master represent? Who is Itisi? Hint! That's a strange name for a dog. I'll turn the sign over now, and let you read the name with spaces. 'It is I.'

"Itisi rebelled against his master so he could go his own way. He didn't want to belong to an owner. Do you ever want to run away so you won't have to obey your parents?

"The master *redeemed* his dog. This means to buy back. When Jesus died on the cross, He made possible our redemption. He didn't wait until we were perfect. Like the dog's master, Jesus accepted us as we are. 'But God shows his love for us in that while we were yet sinners Christ died for us.' "

2 Who Does God Love Most?

Interest Object: Three glasses on a tray

Main Truth: God loves us all the same no matter how bad we are.

Scripture Text: "While we were yet helpless, at the right time Christ died for the ungodly. ... But God shows his love for us in that while we were yet sinners Christ died for us" (Rom. 5:6,8).

Notes and Preparation: To contrast good and bad use a sparkling clean glass of fine crystal and a cheap, obviously dirty, glass of low quality. This second glass can be cracked or purposely stained with chocolate. The third should be an ordinary, clean glass.

"Let's pretend that these three glasses on this tray before you represent children. Some children are very good and others are very bad, but most are just ordinary children. You may decide the best, the worst, and the average child represented by each glass. We want to put them in a line beginning with the worst child of the three. That's easy because we can always point a finger at the worst one. Everyone sees the sins of others and what they have done wrong. Perhaps this child cheats at school or says bad words all the time. He may fight with the other children in his class and do all kinds of mischief. Are we all agreed that this dirty, cracked glass represents the worst child?

"Now let's choose the best child. Again this is easy because this child behaves well in Sunday school and is sometimes the teacher's pet at school. We don't hear about that boy or girl being spanked at home. This beautiful glass represents the best child. Is this your choice?

"Now that we have chosen the worst and the best we have only one left. This glass represents the great majority of children who are good most of the time but sometimes do wrong things. After all, no one is perfect. The Bible teaches us that we are all sinners whom God loves.

"Now we are ready for a very important question. We have already judged which is the worst, the best, and the average. Of these three, which does God love the *most*? [Unless the children have been exceptionally well-grounded in their previous Bible lessons, they will all agree that God loves the best child the most and the worst child the least. Most adults even believe this although they know better. The conclusion should be clearly stated with explanation of the above passage in Romans.]

"In verse 6 we are described as helpless and ungodly. In verse 8 God shows His love not when we become clean and beautiful like the crystal glass, but while we are still sinners. God loves sinners, including the meanest boy or girl. God knows that the worst child can become the best child, so He just loves us all the same way."

3 Straight as a String

Interest Object: Plumb line and children's building blocks

Main Truth: You can't bend God's rules.

Scripture Text: "Then the Lord said, 'Behold, I am setting a plumb line in the midst of my people'" (Amos 7:8).

"Today we have borrowed some building blocks from our church nursery so we can build a brick wall. [As you stack the bricks one on top of another make them purposely out of level so that before you finish construction the wall falls over.] What's wrong here? My brick wall keeps falling down. It doesn't seem to be straight. God's law of gravity cannot be broken. If a wall leans over too far, it will fall over.

"Here is a tool which is one of the oldest building tools known to mankind. It is a string attached to a weight called a plumb. When we hold the string in the air, the heavy weight will pull the string straight. That's where we get the saying 'straight as a string.' Now we can hang the line over the top brick and make the wall straight as a string. With this plumb line we could build a brick building one hundred stories tall and straight as a string so that it would not lean over and fall.

"The plumb line works with God's law of gravity to help keep our buildings and even our sidewalks straight. We can't bend the plumb line because we can't bend God's laws. God has many other laws of right and wrong. We can't change them either. If God says something is wrong, then it is wrong. We can't bend His rules and make it right.

"A long time ago God's prophet Amos lived in a land where God's people were breaking His laws. God appeared to Amos with this vision of a plumb line to remind His people that they would be measured like a wall is measured by a plumb line. If they weren't straight, they wouldn't stand before Him. Wrong would be plain and clear. Punishment would be certain."

4 Sealed by the Holy Spirit

Interest Object: A soft drink bottle and a push down bottle sealer

Main Truth: When Jesus enters your life, the Holy Spirit becomes your seal of protection.

Scripture Text: "And do not grieve the Holy Spirit of God, in whom you were sealed for the day of redemption" (Eph. 4:30).

"Here is a bottle of one of your favorite soft drinks. Let's suppose you drink only half of your pop (or soda) and place the rest of it unopened in the refrigerator. What happens a few days later when you finally decide to drink it? Sure enough. The pop has lost its fizz.

"If we could only seal that bottle, then the fizz would stay inside. That's what this little gadget does. [Hold up bottle sealer.] We can buy it in most any grocery store. When we place it on the top of the bottle and push in, it locks in the contents. We say the bottle is sealed.

"In a similar way we can be sealed by the Holy Spirit. After a person invites Jesus into his or her life, Jesus will stay there forever. He won't slip away, and not even the devil can make Him leave. The Bible describes this as being sealed by the

Spirit. We can think of it as God's lock on our souls so the devil can't break in.

"It is the Holy Spirit who protects us against evil from the outside. 'And do not grieve the Holy Spirit of God, in whom you were sealed for the day of redemption.' "

5 The Unopened Letter

Interest Object:	Colorful envelope
Main Truth:	Don't delay accepting God's invitation.
Scripture Text:	"Behold, now is the acceptable time; behold, now is the day of salvation" (II Cor. 6:2).

Pastor greets the children with Bible in hand. As he begins his lesson a colorful envelope falls to the floor. "What was that? Oh, it's just a letter I received last month. It must be some type of invitation. I really must open it sometime. Looks interesting. [Pastor takes one final brief glance at the envelope and puts it back in his Bible.] Now what was I going to talk about today?

"On second thought, I ought to open that letter now. I think it's from H. Pemrose Hecklemyer. He's the richest boy in town and has all the toys he could ever want. I wish he would ask me over sometime.

"I've heard that he even keeps elephants in his backyard for friends to ride. Wouldn't you like to ride an elephant some day? Doubt if I ever will get to. Oh, well, back to my children's sermon. Let's see now. I need to read something.

"By the way, I hear Pemrose has his own ice cream store. He lets his guests serve themselves. I would take ten scoops of chocolate ice cream and add on marshmallow cream and lots of cherries and whipped cream and nuts. That would really be fun, *if* I could just get an invitation to his house.

At this point some child will surely suggest that the pastor open that envelope right now! It just may be an invitation. "You think so? Could this really be an invitation? I just don't know. [Pastor studies the envelope.] I believe it *is* an invitation.

"Yes, someday I really must open this. It might be an invitation. Oh, you think I should do it now? With all these people around? [After considerable encouragement from the children, the pastor finally tears the envelope open. Sure enough. Here is the long-coveted invitation!]

"Yea, I get to go! I get to go! I have finally been invited. I wonder when it will be. Let's see. It's Saturday. . . . Oh, no! This is terrible! The birthday party was *yesterday*! I waited too long. The party is over. I should have paid more attention.

"Did you know that some people treat God that way? They know that God has good things planned for them—but they put off thinking about God. They have an invitation to accept God, but they wait too long."

6 Sin and Scars

Interest Object:	A piece of white poster board with colored push tacks
Main Truth:	God will remove sins but not the scars.
Scripture Text:	"If we confess our sins, he is faithful and just, and will forgive our sins and cleanse us from all unrighteousness" (I John 1:9).

"Here is a new piece of poster board which has never been used. It looks so nice. Let this poster board represent your life. In my hand are some colored push tacks which we use for bulletin boards. Let these tacks represent the wrongs which we do to God and others in our lives. [Push several tacks into the board.] Every sin mars the poster board and makes it less useful. God is very sad to see our lives so filled with sin.

"We can be thankful that God provided a way for us to be rid of our sins and to be cleansed from them. God can and will remove sins from our lives just as easily as we can pull the tacks from the poster board. In I John 1:9 we read: 'If we confess our sins, he is faithful and just, and will forgive our sins and cleanse us from all unrighteousness.'

"Yes, Jesus will forgive our sins and will cleanse us. That's like pulling out all of these tacks which represent sin. [Pull out the tacks] Now the poster board is clean again. But look carefully. The sin is gone, but the scars remain. This verse speaks about forgiveness and cleansing but *not* about the removing of scars caused by sin. Do you know why God will not remove the scars even though He forgives us and cleanses us from sin? This is His way of reminding us of the pain which our foolishness once caused us.

"I remember as a boy playing with a hot iron. My mother warned me over and over to stop, yet we children were having a little contest. We would place a handkerchief on top of our hand and then put the hot iron on the handkerchief. Then we would see who could wait the longest before the iron began to hurt. I waited too long! The hot iron burned a hole into the handkerchief and right into my skin. I had an ugly sore on my hand for a long time. When the sore finally healed, an ugly scar was left to remind me of my foolishness. Years later people would casually comment, 'What happened to your hand?' How I wished God would remove that scar, but now I understand that it was His way of reminding me of how foolish I had been. The scar kept me from repeating the same mistake.

"Let us always remember that God forgives us. But first we have to be sorry and ask His forgiveness. Then He not only forgives us, but He also cleanses us by removing the sin. God doesn't even remember the sin. But as a warning, the scars remain."

7 The Best Training of All

Interest Object: A jogging shoe, a chessboard, and a Bible

Main Truth: While some train their bodies and others their minds, we must train our souls to be godly.

Scripture Text: "Train yourself in godliness" (I Tim. 4:7b).

"As you were coming to church this morning, perhaps you saw a jogger wearing shoes like this one. Joggers are training their bodies to be strong and healthy. Everyone needs proper exercise to have a strong body, but we need more training than just exercise for the body.

"Here is a chessboard which many people think is the best exercise for training the mind. When you play chess, you must think very hard. It is an excellent game for training the mind to think ahead and concentrate. Yet we need to exercise more than just our body and mind.

"How sad that some people like to train their bodies and others like to train their minds, but so few people realize the importance of training the soul in godly disciplines. We need spiritual exercise just as the jogger needs physical exercise and the thinker needs mental exercise.

"The apostle Paul once explained how training the body is of value, but he said it was more important to 'Train yourself in godliness.' Where do we start? With the Bible. The best exercise for your soul is to read the Bible every day and then to pray to God. Spending much time with God is a good experience which helps you become like God. It's called being godly."

8 Look Inside

Interest Object: An adult trash novel disguised by the cover of a good children's book.

Main Truth: The outside can be disguised but not the inside.

Scripture Text: "Do not look on his appearance ... for the Lord sees not as man sees; man looks on the outward appearance, but the Lord looks on the heart" (I Sam. 16:7).

"Every person ought to read good books, especially in this age of television. The printed word in the book doesn't need commercials or Hollywood stars. If the electricity is out or the television is broken, you can still travel to wonderful places or learn interesting facts from the pages of an open book. Every boy and girl ought to read good books. Notice I said *good* books. Not all books are good. Some have bad language or talk about evil things as if they were good. Other books are wholesome and inspiring. You are a better person when you read good books.

"But how can you tell the difference between a good book and a bad book? Some people read the book cover. This looks like an interesting book which I am holding. The outside cover has pictures of happy children. Now do you think this is a good book?

"If you said, 'Yes,' you are very wrong. We can't tell a book by its outside cover. We must open it and look at a few pages. Wait a minute now. Something is wrong here. As I look on the inside, I see some bad words. Someone has switched book jackets in an attempt to disguise a bad book and make it look good. There is an old saying, 'You can't tell a book by its cover.' How true.

"It is also true that we cannot judge anyone or anything by the outside alone. The Bible teaches us that God does not look on the outside alone but rather on the inside to the heart. The outside is not as important to God as the inside. Remember to fill yourself with good thoughts because God looks within."

9 How to Handle the Truth

Interest Object: Two wrapped boxes

Main Truth: Since God's word is precious, handle it carefully with love and frequent study.

Scripture Text: "Do your best to present yourself to God . . . rightly handling the word of truth" (II Tim. 2:15).

"We have before us two wrapped boxes of equal size. On this first box is a warning: *Fragile: Handle with Care*. What does it mean that something is fragile and needs to be handled with care? You're right. If we drop it, something inside might break. [If the box includes some small expendable glass products, the pastor can 'accidently' drop it. The unmistakable sound of broken glass is effective.]

"Here is a second box which is also wrapped. There is no sign on this box. Let's pretend that dynamite is inside. Now what kind of sign would we need on this package? Yes, *Caution: Explosives* would be a correct sign.

"Since we do not know what is inside this box, we don't really know what kind of label should go on the outside. We can open it now and decide. As you can see, inside is a Bible which is God's word of truth. How should we handle this?

I have a suggestion. We could put a sign which says *Handle with Care.*

"Some people toss their Bible on the table as if it were just another book. The Bible is God's holy word of truth. We should handle it carefully. That doesn't mean we should put it high on a shelf so nothing could happen to it. We should handle it often in loving study of these wonderful words of truth."

10 Tongues and Toothpaste

Interest Object: A tube of toothpaste with a toothbrush

Main Truth: Nothing is so impossible as taking back a spoken word, so be careful.

Scripture Text: "I will guard my ways, that I may not sin with my tongue " (Ps. 39:1).

"Everyone knows that we are supposed to brush our teeth after every meal. You know how to brush your teeth, but how do you correctly squeeze a tube of toothpaste? Some people squeeze in the middle. Let me demonstrate. [The pastor takes the tube and squeezes very firmly from the middle. Out comes a long string of the contents. Then he shows the children how to squeeze correctly from the end of the tube. Out comes even more toothpaste.]

"Now that's the correct way to squeeze the toothpaste, but I have a problem here. I have wasted an awful lot of toothpaste. Will one of you children please put it back in the tube for me? [Let a child try for a minute or so.] You mean it won't go back in? Parents, is that true? Then I am afraid you are right. It's next to impossible having once squeezed the toothpaste out to get it back into that tube.

"That reminds me of something else that can't be done. Nothing is so impossible as taking back the spoken word.

Have you ever said anything when you were very angry and then later felt sorry about saying it? You wish that you could take those words back, but that is as impossible as trying to put toothpaste back into the tube.

"Perhaps you can learn to walk away and count to ten before saying anything when you are angry. Or even better, try repeating this verse from Psalm 39:1: 'I will guard my ways, that I may not sin with my tongue.' If you memorize this and repeat it to yourself, God will help you to keep those harsh words inside. Remember that once you say words, they can't be brought back."

11 Push—Not Pull

Interest Object: Rubber crabs in a bucket

Main Truth: Let us help one another.

Scripture Text: "And as you wish that men would do to you, do so to them" (Luke 6:31).

"Crabs are common little critters who live in the ocean and very often act like boys and girls. Since we don't want to scare anybody, these aren't real crabs. They are made from rubber, but we can pretend that they are alive. Here they are inside this bucket wanting to get out.

"Crabs are not very smart, but then no one needs to be smart to climb out of a bucket this size. A funny thing about a crab is that if he is alone in a bucket, he will eventually climb out. However, if he has other crab friends in the bucket with him, he will never get out. Do you know why? Every time a crab is about to crawl out, one of his friends will grab hold and pull him back in. It seems that every crab wants to be first to get out of the bucket. If he thinks another crab is going to beat him to freedom, he'll grab hold and pull his friend back down.

"How unlike the attitude of Jesus. He taught us to help one another and to love everyone. If these crabs could believe in Jesus, they would treat each other as they want others to treat them. That's the Golden Rule in life.

"There are many different ways to say the same thing. The words we usually quote are 'Do unto others as you would have others do unto you.' My favorite translation is 'Do for others just what you want them to do for you.'

12 Good Punishment

Interest Object: A paddle

Main Truth: Being punished is not all bad if we can learn good lessons.

Scripture Text: "Before I was afflicted I went astray; but now I keep thy word. ... It is good for me that I was afflicted, that I might learn thy statutes" (Ps. 119:67, 71).

"Here is an object which some of you may know about in a very personal way. It is made from wood with one end made to fit a hand. We could call that part a handle. The top part is larger and is certainly not made to fit a hand. It is designed for another part of your body.

"What is this object? Of course, this is a paddle which some teachers call 'the board of education.' Nobody loves a paddle. But I wonder: Is the punishment that this paddle gives good or bad?

"Have any of you ever received a spanking at school? What about at home? Yes, most of you have. Perhaps you suppose that your parents were good and never had whippings. Some children think that pastors are so good they *never* had the paddle applied to them as children.

"The truth is, every child sooner or later disobeys and needs a spanking. We're all human. The only difference between the best children and the meanest children is that the best ones learn quickly from their punishments. They realize how wrong they were and decide not to repeat the bad deeds that caused them to be punished.

"The Bible teaches us that punishment is not always bad. In Psalm 119 we learn, 'Before I was afflicted I went astray; but now I keep thy word. It was good for me that I was afflicted, that I might learn thy statutes.' "

13 On the Level with God

Interest Object: A bubble-type carpenter's level and plain board

Main Truth: If you cannot be honest with God, you cannot be honest with anyone.

Scripture Text: "Therefore, putting away falsehood, let every one speak the truth with his neighbor for we are members one of another" (Eph. 4:25).

"Here is a board which can be nailed to the wall as a shelf for books. In my other hand is a favorite tool of carpenters called a level. I'll explain how it works in just a moment, but first let's see how good your eyes are. If I am nailing this board to the wall, I want it to be very straight or level. Otherwise, something might roll off the shelf. You watch carefully as I hold the shelf in front of you. Tell me when it is straight or level. [With children as with adults, it is difficult to get everyone to agree when the board is perfectly level. At first, make one end obviously higher. When they correct you, drastically tilt it in the opposite extreme. Finally, see if you can please everyone.]

"We do not have to guess if we have this tool. [Hold up the level.] Notice it has a bubble inside the glass tube. This air bubble in the water-filled tube will always rise at an upward direction. You know that is true because when you go swimming and put your head under the water, you can blow air bubbles which rise to the top. All I do to make sure this board is level is to lay this tool on the board and move it until the bubble is exactly in the middle.

"The level is a standard by which we can measure. If the line is to be straight and level, it must match perfectly with the standard. That reminds me of an old saying: 'Are you on the level with me?' That means: 'Are you absolutely truthful with me?'

"God demands that we be truthful with Him. If we cannot tell the truth to God, then how can we be honest with anyone else? We must be on the level with everyone because God expects it. 'Therefore, putting away falsehood, let every one speak the truth with his neighbor, for we are members one of another.' "

14 Magic Beans?

Interest Object: A bag of beans

Main Truth: Not even magic can cancel God's law that we get back what we sow.

Scripture Text: "Do not be deceived; God is not mocked, for whatever a man sows, that he will also reap" (Gal. 6:7).

"Do you know what I have in this bag? These are magic beans! Or at least that's what the stranger told me. He said this new type of bean grows into anything you want. For example, do you children like spinach? [Children usually are quick to refuse any opportunity to associate with spinach!] Well then, how about watermelon? Do you like watermelon? All you need do with these bean seeds is to plant them in the ground and overnight you will have lots of watermelon plants. If you want tomatoes, drop a couple of these special seeds and they grow into tomato plants. It's just that simple with these magic beans.

"Oh, you don't believe me? Now why don't you believe in these magic beans? Of course, you are absolutely right. God has never made any seeds like that. It is a simple law of nature that whatever you plant, that's what you will harvest. If you want corn, then you must plant corn. If you want squash, you can't plant tomato seeds and expect squash.

"This is a truth which even city people can understand.

Although they may never own a garden, they realize they can't grow watermelons from bean seeds. This is one of God's most basic laws here on earth. We harvest what we sow.

"That's certainly true in spiritual life. If you hate everyone, then everyone will hate you. When you refuse to be a friend, others will refuse to be your friend. We get back what we send out.

"It's even more true in our relationship with God. If we do good for God, He does good things for us. We cannot expect God to ignore our sins and then reward us for evil. 'Do not be deceived; God is not mocked, for whatever a man sows, that he will also reap.' "

15 Self-control

Interest Object: Individually wrapped pieces of candy

Main Truth: Better rewards come to those who learn to wait.

Scripture Text: "Every athlete exercises self-control in all things" (I Cor. 9:25).

"Today we will perform an experiment. I want you to learn how to make yourself wait for a better reward later. It's called self-control or will power when we choose to save or wait instead of enjoying something now.

"Each of you may take one piece of this candy which is individually wrapped. Normally you do not eat in church, but this time we will allow it. After you return to your seat, you may eat this candy. But first, listen to my offer. Your parents will cooperate with me, I am sure, because they want you to understand this truth.

"Now this candy may taste good, but it is not really the best kind. In my other sack I have better candy which is sugarless and much bigger. Here is my offer. You may eat your candy now and not have any later. But if you keep your first piece of candy all during the service without unwrapping and eating it, then afterwards I will exchange your little piece for a whole pack of sugarless candy.

"Why should you learn this lesson? It's very important to look ahead and plan. We would have no food for tomorrow if all the farmers stopped planting seeds. Self-control teaches us to delay some of our desires.

"Yet you can never learn self-control until you have full freedom to fail. That's why I give you the opportunity to enjoy a little candy now or a lot more candy later. The choice is yours."

16 Power

Interest Object: A firecracker and a battery

Main Truth: Like a battery a true Christian uses his power to do good with others.

Scripture Text: "But you shall receive power when the Holy Spirit has come upon you; and you shall be my witnesses . . ." (Acts 1:8).

"Here are two common objects both of which have power placed inside them by their makers. They have about an equal amount of power to use as they please. How does the firecracker like to use his power? While the firecracker can deliver a lot of excitement, we must admit that he is a very selfish little character. He wants to do everything all by himself. He tries to be the star of the show by doing what he likes best—blowing up. Sure, he makes lots of noise for a minute. He is a brief flash of light and everyone takes notice. But that's all.

"Some believers in Jesus are like that. At first they get all excited and make a lot of noise. They call much attention to themselves and say, 'Look at me. Look what I have.'

"How unlike the loud firecracker is this quiet, steady, and dependable battery. He doesn't blow up but keeps on working until finally he gives everything he has. He is a steady worker who can last for months and months because he is willing to join with other instruments to be merely the power in the background. He can power a flashlight, a clock, or many of your toys. The battery is a good example of a Christian willing to be a worker and witness for others.

"How will you use the power God gives you? In the Book of Acts we learn about this special power God gives to every believer. What are we supposed to do with this power? 'But you shall receive power when the Holy Spirit has come upon you; and you shall be my witnesses. . . .'

"This is not a once-in-a-lifetime task or a single, selfish moment to explode like a firecracker. It's a long-lasting power to use with God as the main instrument."

17 Something Is Missing

Interest Object: Angel food cake and recipe on paper

Main Truth: Prayer has great power and is greatly missed when absent.

Scripture Text: "The prayer of a righteous man has great power in its effects" (James 5:16).

Notes and Preparation: For this visual effect any box of white cake mix will do. Pour in only one half the mixture and purposely overcook to produce a small and very hard cake.

"Perhaps you have heard the old saying, 'If I knew you were coming I'd have baked a cake.' Well, I knew you were coming today, so I did bake a cake. It has been baking this morning and someone should be bringing it in on a tray right now. Yes, here it comes still in the cake pan which is turned upside down over it.

"I just can't wait to show you this beautiful cake. It will be the biggest, loveliest, lightest cake of all. It's an angel food cake—so light that it may float in the air. Are you ready now to see it? Alright, I will gently lift the cake pan from off the cake. Oh, no! Something bad has happened! I wonder what went wrong. My cake is small and hard as a rock.

"Let me check the directions again. Yes, I added the right amount of flour and cooking oil. Yes, I did put eggs in it. I didn't leave anything out that was important. Nothing, that is, except baking powder. Who would miss a spoon of baking powder?

"Maybe I should ask some mothers present. Is a little baking powder really necessary? [Ladies in the congregation will enjoy answering the pastor on this one!] You mean such a small ingredient makes so big a difference?

"Prayer is like that. It seems so simple just to talk often with God, yet 'The prayer of a righteous man has great power in its effects.' That means God listens most to the person who loves Him and lives the right kind of life."

18 Judgment Day Coming

Interest Object:	A report card
Main Truth:	Rather than trying to avoid judgment we must prepare for it.
Scripture Text:	"It is appointed for men to die once, and after that comes judgment" (Heb. 9:27).

"Every schoolchild knows that teachers are different from other adults. I don't believe they have hidden horns, but I'm still certain they have eyes in the back of their heads. Even when they are writing at the blackboard, they still know what boys and girls are doing behind them.

"Teachers can be found not only in schools but also in church. Will you children look over the congregation with me as we ask all teachers (including those retired or no longer teaching) to raise their hands. Yes, we have teachers present today.

"Let's see if teachers are any different from their pupils. First, I'll ask you students if you like recess? [Children shout yes so pastor turns to teachers in the congregation.] Do you teachers like recess? [They all respond with a hearty yes. You may repeat this process using as your examples lunch periods, assemblies, the last bell of the day, and the last day of the school year.]

"Yes, teachers and students like the same things. Now let's see if they dislike the same things. Do you students like report cards? Of course not. Well, what about you teachers? It appears that teachers don't like report cards any more than their students.

"Report cards are a lot of work for teachers because they have to give tests and then grade papers. Sometimes they must make difficult decisions about reporting bad grades because some students didn't study. Nobody likes report cards. But wait! What about boys and girls who prepared for their studies and therefore received good grades? For those special few who were ready, the day of judgment was not all bad.

"That's how it will be on the last day of this world. God has decided that every person must die sometime and then be judged. How much better for us to be ready!"

19 What Color Is the Rainbow?

Interest Object: Two skeins (or balls) of yarn, one red and the other multicolored, in a sack

Main Truth: Don't argue about who is right because others may truly see something different.

Scripture Text: "Do not judge by appearances, but judge with right judgment" (John 7:24).

"In my sack today I have two skeins of colored yarn. Let me show you the first one. Can you guess its color as I hold it before you? You are right. This is red yarn.

"I won't show you the second skein of yarn yet, but I will choose three children for a little experiment. I have cut three small pieces of yarn from this skein. I will give each of the three children a piece. The pieces are wadded up in my hand so that no one else can see. Take a piece and keep its color a secret. After you have secretly peeped at the yarn, get ready to shout out the color when I count to three. One, two, three! [To the surprise of everyone the three children each shout a different color.]

"Wait a minute! I gave each of you a piece of yarn from the skein. How can you disagree? Are each of you sure? Just so we can settle the matter without argument, please show us your yarn so we can decide for ourselves.

"Look, everyone. Each child is correct. There was no need to argue. But didn't they all receive yarn from the same skein? Let's look at the skein of yarn. Why, it has many colors. You assumed that it must be only one color. That's like arguing about the color of the rainbow. It's many different colors.

"Jesus once reminded us that we should not judge or make decisions by what we see on the outside. Everyone may see something different, and we can each be right in our own ways. He cautioned us to judge instead with 'right judgment.' It's not what we see that counts. It's what God sees that matters."

20 Life the Second Time

Interest Object: Bird nest with eggs inside

Main Truth: Death which ends the first life can lead to a better, second life.

Scripture Text: "I am the resurrection and the life; he who believes in me, though he die, yet shall he live, and whoever lives and believes in me shall never die" (John 11:25-26).

"Here is a bird nest with eggs inside. (Actually, these are not real eggs but let's pretend.) If these were real eggs, we would wonder if they were dead or alive. It's hard to tell just by looking at them. We have to wait until they are hatched. If this were a real egg, we could be sure that inside the egg there is a baby bird growing a little bit each day. He's all cramped up inside that shell, but otherwise he is fine. He has become used to it because he knows nothing else. Toward the end of his life in the shell you can hear him pecking on the walls which enclose him. Soon he will break out to begin a new life.

"Now what would happen if this little bird were afraid to break out? He might think, 'Oh, that would be terrible for me. I cannot leave the nice, comfortable shell which protects me. I'm afraid to go outside.' Perhaps the other baby birds have already hatched and are waiting to play with him, but he doesn't want to leave. Now that would be foolish, wouldn't it? When he finally does peck out of that shell, he makes a wonderful discovery. His new body grows feathers and wings so he can fly. No longer does he live inside his lonely, cramped shell. All the sky is his. He discovers that life the second time around is so much better.

"That experience is similar to our life here on earth. We are cramped inside this earthly body until we can break free to go live in heaven with Jesus. That will be so much better, but most of us are like that little bird. We are afraid to leave this body because death seems so dark.

"Some of you have had a grandparent that died. When you saw the body it was not really your grandfather or grandmother anymore. It was only his (or her) shell. He left it so he could have a better body and live in heaven with Jesus. We, too, will one day have new bodies."

21 The Perfect Tool

Interest Object: A small sack, large enough to insert hand into.

Main Truth: Your hand is a perfect tool and perfect for God's work.

Scripture Text: "But now, O God, strengthen thou my hands" (Neh. 6:9).

Insert one hand into sack and hold sack with other hand.

"As you children are gathering around me, you are naturally very curious about what I have in this sack. Rather than tell you, I will let you guess. But first, here is your only hint. Inside this sack is the world's most important tool. It is perfectly designed to do hundreds of different tasks. Now you may guess. A fork? Hammer? Pencil? No, you are all wrong. Get ready. I'm going to pull from this sack the world's oldest tool, the most perfectly designed and helpful tool mankind has ever known. [Pastor pulls his hand from the sack and holds it up for all to see.]

"That's right. The only tool in this sack was my hand. Have you ever thought of your hand as a perfect tool? You can pick up a small pin, or give a gentle squeeze to affectionately greet someone, or even write a beautiful letter. Dr. Paul Brand, an internationally famous surgeon, says that the hand is absolute, engineering perfection. That means we could not make it better if we tried.

"This skilled surgeon trained his own hands to be expert in repairing the injured hands of others. He has restored many hands through long, delicate operations in which he tied together damaged nerve endings and muscles. When people have accidents and hurt their hands, Dr. Brand often puts their hands back together again. Yet he insists no doctor can improve a normal hand because God has already made it perfect for our use.

"Nehemiah was a great man of God who lived in Old Testament days. He led God's people to use their hands in building a wall around their city. He knew the importance of hands. Once he prayed, 'But now, O God, strengthen thou my hands.' He knew that God made hands not only to build walls but also to do good things for God."

22 Do as I Say?

Interest Object: Hands

Main Truth: Be sure your actions are the same as your words.

Scripture Text: "Little children, let us not love in word or speech but in deed and in truth" (I John 3:18).

"Do you ever wonder what the music director means by waving his arms while everyone is singing? The choir members and some of the people in the congregation know. Maybe someone could explain it to us. [Choose someone to explain.]

Today let's pretend we are a choir, but we won't be singing. I'll use my arms and you watch me closely. First, however, just follow my instructions. Do as I tell you without any help from my hands. Here is what I want you to do: One hand up—Two hands up—One hand down—The other round and round.

"Now some of you did that fine, but you needed a little help. Surely it would be easier if I showed you what I mean. This time follow me with the help of my hands. [Repeat the same procedure and everyone will follow you.]

"Now that you know what I mean, continue to watch me and let's do it again. [This time you say the same words out loud, but when you come to the part "one hand down" you put both hands down. Watch how they all follow your actions

rather than your words.] What happened? My actions con-
fused you. My words said one thing, but my deeds told you
to do something different.

"Let's try another limerick composed by an eleven-year-old
named Craig Bess. First a finger—then a thumb. Tuck in your
tummy, stick out your tongue. [Lead the children in this limerick the first time with correct motions. The second time,
instead of raising a finger first, raise your thumb. Again the
children will follow your actions rather than your instructions.]

"Wouldn't it be a confusing world if everyone gave instructions like that? Here is a lesson to learn. Our deeds ought to
be the same as our words. If I say, 'I love you' then you would
not expect me to kick you in the shins. Our deeds are more
important than our words. This is what the Bible teaches.
'Little children, let us not love in word or speech but in deed
and in truth.'"

23 A Time for Every Purpose

Interest Object: Decorations in a grocery sack

Main Truth: Christmas season is the time for giving.

Scripture Text: "For everything there is a season, and a time for every matter under heaven" (Eccles. 3:1).

Notes and Preparation: This lesson is written for Christmas season, but it can easily be adapted for any time of the year. Just make sure that you begin with the decorations representing the most recent holiday passed and make your application fit the holiday.

"In this sack I have some decorations to help us remember the season we are about to enter. Here is a picture of a turkey representing Thanksgiving. Is now the time to use this decoration on our front door? Of course not. Thanksgiving has just passed, and it is time to go on to the next season. Let's see. What is next? Oh, yes, here it is. We can decorate with this Halloween pumpkin. You mean it is not time for Halloween?

"Well, the Bible says there is a season for everything and a time for every purpose under the heaven. Let's try again with this Easter basket. Or this valentine. All right then, I give up. What season is it? Did you say Christmas? Then we could use this red and green Christmas paper to remind us of the next season.

"Now why would I choose wrapping paper as a reminder of Christmas when a picture of Jesus in the manger or some angels would do just as well? Can you guess?

"Of course, Christmas is the time for gifts. It's fun to receive gifts, but also to give them. For every gift there must be a giver."

24 How to Wake Up

Interest Object: A pillow, bell, and string in a bucket

Main Truth: The best way to wake up in the morning is to think about the good things God will do for you today.

Scripture Text: "This is the day which the Lord hath made; let us rejoice and be glad in it" (Ps. 118:24).

"As you children make your way to the front this morning, you notice I have a pillow and several other items here. One of you may sit down with the pillow on his shoulder. Now, another person can rest your head on the pillow and close your eyes. Pretend you are asleep and that it is time to wake up. For many people waking up is the hardest thing they have to do all day.

"Some people need an alarm clock to wake them up. [Saying this the pastor reaches into the bucket, takes the bell, and rings it in the child's ear.] If you don't like to wake up to the loud noise of a bell ringing in your ears, we could tie a string to your toe and pull you out of bed. Here's a string, but I won't demonstrate that. Everyone knows that a bucket of cold water poured over your head will wake you up in a hurry! Here is the bucket, but we won't pour any water over you this morning.

"Is waking up always that bad? Do you remember some time when you were so excited the night before, you could hardly go to sleep? Perhaps you were going to a big fair or on a vacation leaving early the next morning. You probably woke up quickly that morning!

"That is the answer to the problem of trying to wake up in the morning. Just remember that God has something special for you each day. Think good thoughts about what He will do for you, and you will be excited enough to wake up easily! Catch the excitement of the psalmist who said, 'This is the day which the Lord hath made: let us rejoice and be glad in it.'"

25 Turtles and Tents

Interest Object: A live turtle or a picture of one

Main Truth: Your earthly body is like a house, but a better body awaits you in heaven.

Scripture Text: "For we know that if the earthly tent we live in is destroyed, we have a building from God, a house not made with hands, eternal in the heavens" (II Cor. 5:1).

"Do you like to camp out in the great outdoors? Then you need a tent for your shelter at night. A tent is a temporary house you can carry along with you.

"Of all God's wild creatures, it is obvious that the turtle is best prepared for travel. He never camps out because he's always at home no matter how far he travels. His shell is a house which goes with him always. When he gets tired he can stop and pull himself entirely into his own house and close the doors.

"Like the turtle you and I have a temporary house. The real me lives inside this body. As long as I am alive on this earth, this body is my house or tent. Someday when my time here on earth has ended and God wants me in heaven, I'll leave this body behind and exchange it for a new body in heaven.

"Jesus promised us that He has gone to prepare a place for us in heaven. Since He will be up there, that's where I want to be also. The only way I can get to heaven is to die and leave my body behind here on earth. Sure, I'll hate to see my old house (body) destroyed, but the new building God has for me will last forever."

26 God Sees All

Interest Object: Metal detector and three plastic buckets

Main Truth: God can see everywhere.

Scripture Text: "The eyes of the Lord are in every place, keeping watch on the evil and the good" (Prov. 15:3).

Notes and Preparation: The once mysterious metal detector is now a commonly used tool. If you cannot find one to borrow, a retail store might loan you one for this demonstration. The three plastic buckets need lids and should have no metal handles. Plastic containers for food storage can be used just as well. Line each of these with paper and place silver dollars or other metal treasure inside one container.

"Would you children like to go on a treasure hunt with me? Here is a metal detector which can find buried treasure. I don't understand how it works, but I've used it. Since we can't leave the worship service right now, I have brought buried treasure here. Or perhaps we should call it sealed treasure because it's in one of these three containers.

"How can we decide which one has the treasure? With our eyes we cannot see through most objects, so I'll turn on the metal detector and point it toward the first container. Nothing happens which means it has no metal treasure inside.

Remove the lid to be sure. Let's try the second container. Again, nothing happens. We open the second container and find it empty. I hope it will be in this last container. Listen to the noise the metal detector makes. Yes, we have found the treasure. Inside are some silver dollars.

"While we could not see through the containers, this instrument was able to find the treasure easily. If a machine made by man can see better than our eyes, we can be certain that God who made everything sees everywhere.

"God sees both the good and the evil done by people. There is no place where we can hide from His watchful eye. The Bible says, 'The eyes of the Lord are in every place, keeping watch on the evil and the good.'"

27 Trust in the Lord

Interest Object:	Small box or footstool
Main Truth:	We must trust in God and not be afraid
Scripture Text:	"I will trust, and will not be afraid; for the Lord God is my strength and my song, and he has become my salvation" (Isa. 12:2).

"You have all heard the old saying, 'It's as easy as falling off a log.' If you have ever climbed around on logs, you know they may be slippery and sometimes will roll when you are walking on them. It's very easy to slip and fall off a log.

"Today I don't have a log, but this stool will do just as well. I will ask this boy to help me demonstrate this lesson. Because it is so easy to fall off a log, let's make it more difficult. I want you to fall off this log backwards. Now my helper is shaking his head saying he doesn't want to fall off backwards. Perhaps I should explain. I will be behind you and will catch you. That sounds easy, doesn't it? But it's not. Even though he knows I will be behind him, and I have promised to catch him, it is still very hard to fall off backwards."

(The pastor should practice this procedure before the Sunday presentation. Even though your own son or daughter trusts you completely, the first few times he tries, the body will instinctively react and overrule that element of trust. Even as the child falls backwards, he begins to reach out his arms preparing for the fall.)

"This is really a frightening experience the first time you try. It requires complete trust. You know I love you and have promised to catch you, but still it is hard not to be afraid. You must trust your body into my hands. That is called faith and is a good example of how God wants us to trust Him.

"The best way to live in the world is simply to trust God always. Isaiah said, 'I will trust, and will not be afraid; for the Lord God is my strength and my song, and he has become my salvation.'"

28 All Treasure and No Trash

Interest Object: Discarded aluminum cans

Main Truth: God makes no trash but everything on earth has value.

Scripture Text: "The earth is full of thy riches" (Ps. 104:24 KJV).

"Here is an empty soft drink can which some litterbug carelessly dropped on our church lawn. That's wrong, but whoever threw away this can was wrong on something else too. He treated this can like trash and did not know how valuable it really is. This can is made of 100% aluminum which can be reused. Many people will buy it from us for recycling. At today's prices it's worth one penny per can. Find four more cans and you will have a nickel or ninety-nine and you will have a dollar.

"A penny may not sound like much, but pennies add up to make great riches. If you had $999,999.99 you would not be a millionaire. Add just this can worth one penny, and indeed you would be a millionaire!

"Yes, this can is very valuable as treasure, not trash. But after all, God made everything with value and purpose. That is the lesson a boy once learned in Sunday school. He came out of his class very happy saying, 'God made me and I'm okay because God don't make no trash!' That's so true.

"Look around, 'The earth is full of thy riches.' Just because some items are thrown away doesn't mean they are worthless. With a little ambition you can turn cans into cash the way others turn paper into profit. They call it recycling, but we can think of it as treasure, not trash."

29 Strangers to the Spirit

Interest Object: A Spanish Bible

Main Truth: Without the Spirit you cannot understand things of the Spirit.

Scripture Text: "The unspiritual man does not receive the gifts of the Spirit of God, for they are folly to him, and he is not able to understand them" (I Cor. 2:14).

"As we begin, hear God's Word which I read for you. 'El que no es espiritual no accepta las cosas que son del Espiritude Dios, porque para el son tonterias.'

"What's wrong? Don't you understand spiritual words? [The children will not let you get by with this. They know you weren't reading English.] Then what language was I reading? You're right. It was Spanish, and unless you understood that language you could not know what I was saying. Spanish uses the same alphabet, many similar sounds, and some of the same words as English. But without an understanding of the language, Spanish sounds like gibberish.

"Perhaps you boys or girls will start a secret boys' or girls' club some lazy summer day. After you choose a name for your club and find a secret hideout, you choose a mysterious password which is kept secret from outsiders. Unless you're in the club, you won't understand what is going on or even be able to get in.

"Church seems like that to outsiders even though we aren't trying to keep secrets from people. We build our churches with big doors and paint the word *Welcome* over them so everyone can enter. Yet the outsider who doesn't know Jesus or have His Spirit just can't understand us. And no wonder! Even our language is different from clubs, sport teams, or businesses. We talk about love, giving, sacrifice, and a cross. Our behavior is not always the same as what people in a selfish world follow.

"How sad that so many are strangers to our Spirit. They can't understand our language of love anymore than we can understand a foreign language. But if they become one of us by belonging to Jesus, then they won't be outsiders. God will teach spiritual truths to them.

"Now let me read in English that same verse I read earlier from the Spanish Bible. 'The unspiritual man does not receive the gifts of the Spirit of God, for they are folly to him, and he is not able to understand them.' "

30 Give Up?

Interest Object: A Chinese fingertrap

Main Truth: Sometimes we must give up and surrender before we can get out and get along.

Scripture Text: "We ceased and said, 'The will of the Lord be done'" (Acts 21:14).

Notes and Preparation: A Chinese fingertrap can be found in many novelty stores or at the midway of any carnival. Remember the secret of this little trap. As long as you fight it and pull hard, you can't get your finger loose. When you relax the pressure, the woven straw contracts in length and expands around your finger. Then you can slide out the trapped finger.

"Sometimes when boys and girls wrestle or fight, one may get the other trapped. The winner refuses to release his friend until that person says calf-rope or uncle. With those words the player who is defeated admits that he cannot win. He gives up and the game is over.

"That's how you can play the game with this Chinese fingertrap. You put the index finger of one hand into one end and then your other index finger into the other end. Now quickly try to pull your fingers out. The harder you pull the tighter the fingertrap holds. The only way you can get out of this Chinese fingertrap is to admit defeat and quit pulling so hard. Then it will let you loose.

"Some boys and girls want so very much to please God. They try and try. Then one day they do something wrong and realize how hard it is to be perfect. They feel bad. What can they do? The only honest thing is to say to God, 'I'm sorry. I give up. I tried but I failed.'

"At that point, a miracle happens. When you give up in submission to God, then God helps you. Soon you are able to resist the trap into which you had earlier fallen.

"One day at the beach a teen-ager swam far out into the deep water. He was having lots of fun until he tried to swim back. Then he realized he had gone too far and had no strength left. He was about to drown when a lifeguard saw the danger. The lifeguard plunged into the water, swam all the way out to the drowning young man, and tried to help him. The young man was so frightened that he resisted the efforts of his rescuer. Thrashing in the water he would swing his arms back and forth and try to hold on to the lifeguard. As a result both the lifeguard and the foolish swimmer nearly drowned.

"Do you know what the wise lifeguard did? He swam away just a few feet and waited until the drowning man had exhausted all his strength. Then just as he was about to go under for the last time, the lifeguard swam closer, grabbed hold, and pulled the limp body back to shore and safety.

"So often, we try to do things our own way. Only when we give up can we learn what faith really means. Some friends of Paul learned this kind of faith. The Bible describes it: "We ceased and said, 'The will of the Lord be done'" (Acts 21:14)."

31 Giving Back to God

Interest Object: Ten artificial flowers in a vase

Main Truth: You can't give to God what is already His, but you can give back to Him what He has given to you.

Scripture Text: "For every beast of the forest is mine, the cattle on a thousand hills. I know all the birds of the air, and all that moves in the field is mine" (Ps. 50:10-11).

"Here are ten lovely flowers in a vase. Let's pretend that I have grown these flowers in my front yard and you come along to admire them. You want them for yourself and take one. Is that good? No, that's stealing.

"But suppose I see you admiring the flowers and walk out to greet you saying, 'Pick as many flowers as you want.' That would be nice so you pick ten of my flowers. That's not stealing because the owner is giving them away. But after you leave, you remember your manners. You forgot to thank me, so you return and bring me a nice surprise. You give me one of the flowers I had grown.

"Now let's think about this. You can't really give me a flower because it was mine anyway. In this case, you are giving *back* to me. We must always remember this important difference. We can't give anything to God (He already owns everything), but we can give *back* to Him in gratitude what He has given to us.

"The Bible teaches that God owns everything. 'For every beast of the forest is mine, the cattle on a thousand hills. I know all the birds of the air, and all that moves in the field is mine.' God is already rich beyond measure. He doesn't need our gifts, but He does want us to be thankful and generous. The best way is giving *back* to God from the abundance He has already given to us."

32 You Can't Hide from God

Interest Object:	Halloween mask
Main Truth:	Since God knows you anyway, you can't hide from Him behind a mask.
Scripture Text:	"Man looks on the outward appearance, but the Lord looks on the heart" (I Sam. 16:7).

As the children gather around the pastor, they notice he has a sack. He explains that he wants to try an experiment. Will they all close their eyes for just a moment? When all the eyes are closed, he pulls a Halloween mask out of the sack and puts it on. The children open their eyes, giggle, and point at the pastor who now tries to disguise his voice.

"Good morning, children. Your pastor had to leave while you closed your eyes. Although I am a stranger here, maybe I can tell you a story. What's the matter? Why are you laughing at me? You don't know me. I'm not your pastor. [At this point the children will be insistent. It's no use trying to fool them. The mask doesn't do any good. They already know their pastor too well, so he removes the mask.]

"I suppose that was rather ridiculous of me, wasn't it? You are impossible to fool because you know me too well. The Halloween mask just didn't work. However, I remember one boy on Halloween night who was surprised when his neighbors did not recognize him. When he rang their doorbell and shouted 'Trick or Treat' they laughed at this stranger and gave him some candy. But it was obvious that they did not know who he was. Well, if they didn't recognize him, perhaps he could have more fun. He knocked over their lawn chair and kicked to pieces their pumpkin. They yelled, 'Little boy, you stop that!' He ran away confident that they could not tell his parents because they did not recognize him.

"He did lots of bad things that night. With his Halloween mask he was safe. He was having so much fun. Then he remembered the words of his Sunday school teacher. The lesson the previous Sunday was about how God made us, loves us, and will always recognize us. He began thinking. Even though his neighbors did not recognize him, God knew who he was. No one can fool God.

"The Bible says, 'Man looks on the outward appearance (which is what the neighbors saw—his mask), but the Lord looks on the heart.' We can't hide anything from God. The next day the boy apologized to his neighbors and asked God to forgive him."

33 What's Inside?

Interest Object: A lump of coal

Main Truth: Both good and bad thoughts can come from deep within the heart, so be careful.

Scripture Text: "Keep your heart with all vigilance; for from it flow the springs of life" (Prov. 4:23).

"This black rock I am holding is really a lump of common coal which can be burned in a stove as fuel. For hundreds of years people have used coal to keep warm without ever realizing the many uses it has locked inside.

"Coal is dug from the ground. Rather than being a rock it is the hard-pressed remains of grass, weeds, and leaves from thousands of years ago. From coal is squeezed a tar substance which is remarkable for its many uses. Can you imagine this lump of coal being used to make perfume, plastics, or food preservatives?

"Here is a list of other things that can be made from coal: vitamins, paint thinner, linoleum, moth balls, saccharin, synthetic rubber, nylon, ammonia, fertilizer, aspirin, sulphur, and a rainbow of many different dyes. These are all good things stored inside this lump of coal.

"On the other hand, scientists can also produce from coal many poisons, harmful drugs, poisonous gas, and even bombs. Imagine all of that from this innocent-looking lump of coal!

"The Bible teaches that our hearts inside are very similar

to coal. Deep within the heart can be stored both good and evil. That's why we must be very careful what we hear and read. The heart is the storehouse of all of our thoughts and deeds. We must be careful about what goes in and what comes out.

"Long ago a wise man included in a proverb this same warning. We are to guard the thoughts of our hearts. 'Keep your heart with all vigilance; for from it flow the springs of life.' "

34 Beautiful Feet

Interest Object: A very big shoe

Main Truth: All feet are beautiful when they are going to tell others about Jesus.

Scripture Text: "How beautiful are the feet of those who preach good news!" (Rom. 10:15).

"Look at this big shoe! Can you imagine how big the feet are of those wearing this size? Would you call feet this big beautiful? Of course not. We just don't think of feet as being beautiful.

"Nowadays, we seldom notice feet because everyone wears shoes. In Bible days, however, people either went barefoot or wore sandals. When you entered a home after a long walk over dusty roads, your host would not visit until he looked at your feet to see how dusty they were. Then he would command his servants to bring some water and towels to clean your dirty feet. First things first! They wanted you to be comfortable in much the same way parents want to help you remove wet boots on the porch before entering the house.

"If we meet someone today whom we haven't seen for years, we often say, 'I'm sure glad to see your face!' In the Bible days they said, 'Am I glad to see your feet!'

"Now I have a question for you. How do you make your feet beautiful? Women put makeup on their faces and both men and women dress up in nice clothes to look good. But besides buying new shoes, is there a way to make your feet beautiful?

"This subject sounds funny, but the Bible gives us a serious formula for making our feet beautiful. Listen as I read from Romans when Paul quoted the Old Testament prophet Isaiah, 'How beautiful are the feet of those who preach good news!'

"There you have it! Your feet can be beautiful if you use them to go tell others about the Good News of Jesus. No matter how big, or flat, or strange your feet may look, they can be beautiful."

35 How to See Yourself?

Interest Object: A black cardboard tube open on both ends plus a small mirror

Main Truth: Like a mirror which helps us to see our outside appearance, the Bible shows us what's inside.

Scripture Text: "For the word of God is living and active ... discerning the thoughts and intentions of the heart" (Heb. 4:12).

Notes and Preparation: For this funny experiment you need only a common cardboard tube open on both ends. Spray paint it black. Just before the presentation dip both ends in black powder or a washable liquid. Test it to be sure the tube leaves the telltale ring around one's eye after looking through it. Choose a favorite adult member in advance and secretly explain this old gag. Let him be a real ham who will leave a good impression.

"With this interesting tube we can see strange spots and circles. Let's choose an adult who can demonstrate how it works. [Make it appear you pick someone at random. He raises it to his eyes, looks with curiosity, and then reports that he sees nothing. As soon as he lowers the tube, the children laugh at the ring left around his eye. He supposedly remains unaware of this trick.]

"Sir, you mean you don't see anything? Let me ask the children if they see strange circles. [They enthusiastically answer in the affirmative.] Perhaps, sir, you ought to look with the other eye. [The same experience is repeated. Then you can suggest he place it on his forehead and look through his 'mind's eye.' He will wind up with circles everywhere!]

"I suppose it is time we let our helper in on this little secret. Sir, with that tube you can't see what's on the outside. You need a mirror. Look inside.

"While our assistant goes to wash his face, let me explain. Like a mirror which helps us to see our outside appearance, so the Bible shows us what's inside. 'For the word of God is living and active ... discerning the thoughts and intentions of the heart.' "

36 First Fruits or Last Crumbs?

Interest Object: A sliced, imitation cake

Main Truth: God deserves to be remembered first instead of last.

Scripture Text: "The first of the first fruits of your ground you shall bring into the house of the Lord your God" (Exod. 23:19).

Notes and Preparation: The extra preparation for this timely truth is well worth the effort. Cut from poster board six signs about 6×18 inches and attach string so they can be hung around the necks of children. On each sign write a different expense as follows: house—30%, food—30%, auto—20%, clothing—10%, and miscellaneous—10%. The sixth sign is labeled *Church*. A round cake can be cut from styrofoam and further cut into five slices to equal the personal expenses of an average family. If the styrofoam is white it can be stained with spray paint or liquid shoe polish for a dark color.

The pastor begins by welcoming a church member who brings the signs. He or she greets the children, choosing five of them to line up in order each wearing a sign. The pastor wears the sixth sign representing the church. He stands to the side while the assistant explains.

"God allows us to work for money which we then exchange for our basic needs and wants. This piece of cake represents the wages a family might earn and is thus cut into several slices. The child whose sign says *house* is given the first slice. We must have shelter, you know. Then the second child receives *food.* Everyone needs to eat."

At this point the pastor interrupts and wonders when God's church will receive a gift. The assistant comforts him by saying, "Just wait, pastor. I have something for the church. But next we must remember that an automobile is very important. We must somehow get to work, school, and to church. Here is some for *auto.* The procedure is continued with the pastor becoming more nervous as he watches the cake disappear. Will there be anything left for the church? Finally, the truth is known. After all the bills are paid there is *nothing* left but a few crumbs for God and His church.

The assistant apologizes while the pastor recites the verse: 'The first of the first fruits of your ground you shall bring into the house of the Lord your God.' This means God comes first. He deserves more than just the leftover crumbs of our prosperity."

37 Time for Beauty

Interest Object: Geodes in a sack

Main Truth: Beautiful things are often overlooked because we don't take time to look within.

Scripture Text: "He has made everything beautiful in its time" (Eccles. 3:11).

"As you are taking your place here around me, let me remind you that God has made a beautiful world. The Bible says, 'He has made everything beautiful in its time.' I have asked our guest,————to bring some objects of beauty that come from God's great outdoors. He is a geologist [or rock hound if no geologists are available. Explain what He does.] He is often outside, so I have asked him to bring some special object of beauty. Are you ready,————?"

Guest: "Pastor, inside this sack are some rocks of great beauty. [The guest then reveals what appears to be round, ugly rocks. The pastor reacts immediately suggesting that his guest did not understand the request. We wanted some special rocks which God has touched with beauty.] Now pastor, practice what you preach! The Bible says that God has made everything beautiful in its time. That means we must take time to examine these rocks carefully. Notice that there is a rubber band around each one. Each of these rocks has been cut in half. Look inside. [The children and pastor will gasp as the ugly rocks are opened to reveal beautiful crystal formations inside.]"

Pastor: "I have just learned a lesson. We must take time to see beauty in everything. And not just rocks. Some people, for example, don't understand that prayer time with God is beautiful. They think it's wasted time which they could better use for playing ball or watching television. But like these rocks, our prayers with God become very beautiful when we take time."

38 Trained by Patience

Interest Object: Violin or other musical instrument

Main Truth: Only through personal practice can we learn to make beautiful music, to know right from wrong, and to grow spiritually.

Scripture Text: "For those who have their faculties trained by practice to distinguish good from evil" (Heb. 5:14b).

Notes and Preparation: In this lesson the musical instrument chosen is not important, but you do need the assistance of a member who has mastered the instrument. Your assistant can be seated on a nearby pew.

"Children, today I'm very excited because I have a violin given to me by————. She has played this beautiful instrument for many people through the years, but now she is willing for me to have it. The violin is the most delicate and sensitive of all musical instruments. Would you like me to play it?

(The children naturally agree so the pastor begins to build the suspense. With a dramatic flair he tucks the violin under his chin and lifts the bow ready to play. Then he pauses to talk some more. The process is repeated again so that everyone is doubly eager to hear him. When at last he finally draws the bow across the strings, it's not beautiful music but an awful noise. With a strange and frustrated look on his face, he asks "What is wrong?" This violin must be broken because it won't play. All his life he had been waiting to play a violin and now when his big moment comes, this must be a broken violin.)

[At this point the owner of the instrument rescues the pastor and explains to the children about personal discipline.] "Although it looks easy for some people to play the violin, it is only because they are experts who have practiced for years learning to make beautiful music. The musician plays a few bars of music. [Then the pastor summarizes the lesson by application to spiritual matters.] We can't one day decide to be the best person around without some serious work on it. We must discipline ourselves in learning right from wrong. That is the meaning of the verse in Hebrews 5:14 describing mature believers who have been trained by practice and discipline."

39 Trees for Toothpicks and Telephone Poles

Interest Object: A pinecone, acorn, or small potted tree

Main Truth: God has a purpose for every person on earth.

Scripture Text: "And the Lord God planted a garden in Eden, in the east: and there he put the man whom he had formed. And out of the ground the Lord God made to grow every tree that is pleasant to the sight and good for food. . . " (Gen. 2:8-9).

Notes and Preparation: If you like to involve lay members or invited guests, a forest ranger in uniform is the ideal expert. However, almost anyone can consult a book and present interesting facts about trees.

"Today we have a special guest who can tell us much about trees. I suppose he will start with what everyone knows. There are little trees and there are big trees. From the little trees we get toothpicks, and from the big trees we get telephone poles. Right?"

Guest: "Well, pastor, there's more to trees than that. Between little trees and big trees God has given us thousands of different sized trees, and each has a special purpose. Here is an acorn from an oak tree which is useful for firewood and for fine furniture. This seed can grow into a mighty oak, or it can be eaten as food by squirrels, deer, and even pigs.

"Now as for toothpicks and telephone poles, they come usually from pine trees grown from this pinecone. Only 1 percent of pine trees harvested for wood ever become telephone poles or even fence posts.

"One half of all the wood cut in America is used for lumber in buildings. Yet we need not wait for some trees to grow big because at half grown they are just right for pulp wood. We grind the wood, mix it with water, cook it, and make paper for books, newspapers, letters, and cardboard boxes."

Pastor: "Thank you, ———, for telling us about trees. The part I liked best was your emphasis that God has a purpose for every tree no matter what its size. That's true for people, too. No matter how small or young we may be, God loves us and has a special purpose for us in life.

"Come to think of it, God has always put people and trees together. In the very first book of the Bible we are told about the garden of Eden and the first trees which God planted. Let's read that passage right now."

40 The Whole Armor of God

Interest Object: Fireman wearing full gear

Main Truth: As a fireman who battles fire needs proper equipment, so Christians need spiritual armor to fight the devil.

Scripture Text: "Put on the whole armor of God, that you may be able to stand against the wiles of the devil" (Eph. 6:11).

"Today we have as our guest Mr.————who is all dressed up for work. [If no fireman is available, bring items of clothing worn by fireman, or a picture.] There's no doubt about his occupation. We have invited this fireman to visit with us and explain his outfit. Mr.————, say hello to our children, and then tell us why you are dressed this way. You might begin with your boots. Since it is not raining outside today, why are you wearing boots?"

Guest: "Pastor, it may be hot and dry when we go to fight fires, but at most fires we use fire hoses to put water on the flames. You notice I also have a raincoat which gives me protection from both fire and water. Both the boots and the raincoat are rubber on the outside but lined on the inside with material that will not burn.

"My hat is not a regular hat but is like a soldier's heavy

helmet. It protects me from falling debris like rocks, glass, or burning boards. Finally, the oxygen tank on my back and the mask for my face let me breathe inside a smoky room. So just about everything a fireman wears is like armor which protects him so he can do his job in dangerous circumstances."

Pastor: "Thank you, Mr. Fireman, for that explanation. I'm also glad that you used an interesting word describing what you wear. You said it was like armor. We Christians are familiar with that word. Paul, writing to the Ephesians, warned, 'Put on the whole armor of God, that you may be able to stand against the wiles of the devil.' He explained that the Christian needs armor to fight against the devil, but our armor is spiritual in nature. We are to put on a breastplate of righteousness, to use the shield of faith, and wear a helmet of salvation. With the whole armor of God, we can stand against the devil's tricks."

41 Brave as a Lion

Interest Object: A policeman

Main Truth: A clear conscience has no fear.

Scripture Text: "The wicked flee when no one pursues, but the righteous are bold as a lion" (Prov. 28:1).

As the children gather around the pastor he introduces his policeman friend and asks them to all say hello to the officer.

"Let's talk about a policeman's job. Can you guess what his duties are? [Don't worry. These children will respond with many observations including how the policeman not only protects us from bad people, but also helps lost children find their way home, directs traffic, helps during accidents, etc.]

"Yes, we're usually glad to see a policeman. We smile and wave at him and hope that he will wave back. But is there ever a time when someone would not want to see a policeman? The crook or robber never wants to see a policeman. Let's ask the policeman, 'How do you know when someone has done something bad?' "

Guest: "Guilty people seldom wave at a policeman. They usually turn around and try to hide. Sometimes they run away from us when we aren't even chasing them. That's when we suspect they are guilty."

Pastor: "I remember a Scripture verse that describes this very thing. 'The wicked flee when no one pursues. . . .' That's because they have a guilty conscience. They are afraid of being caught.

"There is a good way never to be afraid of a policeman and never to have a bad conscience. The best way to avoid worrying about anything you have done wrong is simply: Don't do anything wrong! You can be brave as a lion if you are honest. A clear conscience has no fear.

"Let's read the rest of that verse. 'The wicked flee when no one pursues, but the righteous are bold as a lion.' "

42 The One-eyed Monster

Interest Object: Picture of a television

Main Truth: Be careful what you watch on television.

Scripture Text: "If then you have been raised with Christ, seek the things that are above, where Christ is, seated at the right hand of God. Set your minds on things that are above. . . ." (Col. 3:1-2).

"Children and pets just seem to go together. How many of you have pets? Can you name them for me? [Children respond by naming a great variety of pets.] I have in mind one pet which all of you know about but which no one mentioned. Listen to this story about a one-eyed monster pet.

"There once lived a happy family who had many different pets. They had dogs, cats, turtles, mice, and even goldfish. Then one day the father brought home an exciting new pet different from any other. It was not an outside pet but one which barged right into their home, chose its own special corner, and became very jealous of everyone's attention. Every family member had to gather around close and spend hours of time with it. Even when neighbors dropped by, this pet would not be silent but dominated everything. Soon friends and neighbors stopped visiting in the home of that family.

"What was this new pet like? Instead of having two eyes like other pets, it had only one eye. That's why they called it a one-eyed monster. Yet it could do some things very well. This new pet entertained the children for hours with games and stories. They laughed and laughed and even learned some very good lessons.

"Unfortunately, they also learned some very bad things. The new pet told them terrible stories and taught them bad words. Sometimes the children would have nightmares after being entertained by the monster. Their schoolteachers could not understand why they seldom did their homework or their grades fell.

"What kind of monster pet was this new creature? By now you can probably guess that it was a television set. I hope that you will be careful of that persistent pet in your home. Remember it has a little knob which you can use. It's the off button."

43 The Magic Glasses

Interest Object: Ordinary eyeglasses

Main Truth: You can see good in others if you try.

Scripture Text: "And there was much muttering about him among the people. While some said, 'He is a good man,' others said, 'No, he is leading the people astray'" (John 7:12).

"This is a story about a man nobody liked. He didn't have a friend in the world. Even his own family didn't like him. You know why? He could never see good in others. Instead of thinking good thoughts about people, he criticized and thought the worst about others.

"His son was discouraged. When he brought home a report card with all B's, his dad said: 'Why didn't you make A's? What's wrong with you?'

"He complained about his wife's cooking. He never had anything nice to say to her.

"Do you think that man was happy? Of course not. He was so miserable that one day an angel appeared and promised to help him with magic glasses. 'They will let you see secret things of good about others. You will be very happy, but tomorrow I must have these glasses back.'

"Well, the man was excited that at last he could be happy. On his way home he saw an old woman stumble and fall. Without those magic glasses, he would have said: 'Old woman, why are you so clumsy? Get out of my way!' But he didn't. Now he could see that she had slipped on a banana peel dropped by a thoughtless child. He helped her up and was rewarded by her smile which made him even more happy.

"He arrived home to see his son in the yard playing ball with a neighbor boy. The son thought, 'Oh, no, Dad is going to complain about our playing on his beautiful lawn.'

"But the father remembered the magic glasses and looked carefully to see that the friend was crippled. The other children seldom played with him, but his own son was taking the time. Thus he said, 'Hello, boys. I see you're enjoying yourselves. Be careful about the grass, but do have a good time!'

"The family was excited and happy about the change. Then the man began to worry about returning the glasses the next day. That made him sad. Could he ever be happy again?

"Surprise! The angel returned and told him a secret. The glasses were not really magic. Anyone who was willing to try could learn to see good in others. He was willing. From then on he was the best friend, husband, and dad ever because he had learned the secret. Anyone who is willing can see good in others.

"Do you know where the angel learned this truth? He remembered how people watched Jesus doing good. The Bible says that they did not all agree about Jesus. 'While some said, "He is a good man," others said, "No, he is leading the people astray." '

"So there we have it. There are two types of people. Those who see good in others and those who don't. Which are you?"

44 Tell the Whole World

Interest Object: A large Hershey bar and small bite-sized bars for the children

Main Truth: Jesus depends on satisfied customers, not paid salesmen, to tell others about Him.

Scripture Text: "You shall be my witnesses" (Acts 1:8).

Notes and Preparation: For a special treat consider giving each child a bite-sized Hershey bar. Be sure to have napkins handy and a wastebasket for the paper wrappers.

"Would you like to enjoy a Hershey bar while I tell you the story about Mr. Milton Hershey? Two things Mr. Hershey always loved were children and chocolates. Believing that the two ought to go together, in 1903 he started a chocolate factory in rural Pennsylvania. Making good chocolate was not really that difficult. The hard part was to get out and sell the chocolate. Experts told him that the only way he could sell his chocolate bars would be to pay people to tell others. This is called advertising.

"Of course, advertising does help sell products. For example, whenever a toy company comes out with a new doll or space toy, they tell about it on television. That costs a lot of money so they usually raise the price of their product to include advertising. Mr. Hershey refused to do this. He said,

"If my product is good, people will tell others who will also buy my product. The new people will then tell even more people." That is exactly what happened. For years and years the Hershey candy bar was the only nationally enjoyed product in America which was never advertised on radio or in the magazines. Mr. Hershey was a very smart man. He was also a good man who used his profits to build an orphanage which has helped raise thousands of children since then.

"Let me ask you now. Was your bite-sized Hershey bar very good? Of course it was! When you return to your seat your brother or your parents may ask you, 'Was it good?' Surely you would not expect money from me for you to tell the truth. You are a satisfied customer. So I don't need to pay you to advertise what you already like.

"If you believe in Jesus, you know that He is the most wonderful person in the world. Jesus doesn't need to pay for advertising. You will want to tell others about Him. And that's the last commandment He left His disciples, 'You shall be my witnesses.' He did not say, 'You shall be paid to be my witnesses.' "